Wilderness World

Fishing

To Derek, Matt, and Zachary

May you be free and happy
in the wilderness world

Wilderness World

Fishing

by Paul Neimark
illustrations by Tom Dunnington
Created by Zachary's Workshop LTD
Consulting Editor
Tom Opre
Midwest Field Editor
Field & Stream Magazine

 CHILDRENS PRESS, CHICAGO

Picture Acknowledgements:
U.S.D.A.—U.S. Forest Service—pages 14, 21, 22, 25, 26-27, 32, 34-35, 36, 40, 44, 46-47, 48, 50, 54, Front Cover
COURTESY TRAVEL BUREAU, MICHIGAN DEPARTMENT OF COMMERCE— pages 8, 10, 13, 28, 42

Library of Congress Cataloging in Publication Data

Neimark, Paul G
  Fishing.

  ((Wilderness world)
  SUMMARY: Explains the basic techniques of fishing.
  1. Fishing—Juvenile literature. 1. Fishing]
I. Dunnington, Tom. II. Zachary's Workshop.
  III. Title. IV. Series.
SH445.5.N44   799.1'1   80-27508
ISBN 0-516-02452-3

Contents

Chapter 1

How Do You Catch Fish?

Jill and Tom both went fishing one Saturday morning, but not with each other. At the end of the day, Jill brought home six big fish. She froze four of them. Her family ate the other two for dinner. They were delicious!

Tom came home the way he went out — with no fish. Why did Jill do so well? Why did Tom "get skunked?"

There are several reasons, but there is really one simple explanation. Jill knew and practiced a few simple fishing rules. Tom didn't.

This book will tell you some of the basic facts about fishing. You will learn how to look for good

Opposite: Fishing with a friend is safer — and much more fun!

fishing spots, the different kinds of bait, what to do when you have a nibble, and what to do after you catch the fish.

You can fish in many different ways. On the ocean you can catch enormous tuna, bonito, or other salt-water fish from a boat. You can fish underwater with a spear or net. You can fish in lakes or streams with a casting rod and reel. Jill and Tom used the easiest method, some bait tied to the end of fishing line hanging from a pole. That is called *stillfishing* or *pole fishing*. It is the method you will read about in most of this book. Once you master this way to fish, you will know so much that the other methods will be easier.

Of course, you cannot learn everything about fishing from a book. You need to practice, and the more practice you get, the better you will be at fishing. Other fishermen — men, women, boys, and girls — can tell you a lot, too. They know what kinds of fish live in your area, what kinds of bait to use, and where the best fishing spots are.

You might hear fishermen say that they know this or that "secret" about how to catch fish. But all in all, the difference between catching fish and not catching fish comes down to simple things. The first is: Know where the fish are. . . and fish when they are hungry.

Opposite: You don't need a boat to go shallow-water fishing. You do need to be extra-careful not to fall.

Chapter 2

Where the Fish Are

Fishermen who really know what it's all about like to tell a story about a man who lost a dollar one night. He was searching under a bright street lamp when a friend came by and asked what he was doing. "I've been here over an hour," the fellow said, "looking for a dollar that fell out of my pocket."

"An hour is a long time," his friend said. "Where did you lose the money?"

The fellow answered, "Half a block down. But the light is better here."

In the same way, too many would-be fishermen — and Tom was one of them — don't go where the fish are, but where the "light is better." Tom went to a

Opposite: A fish's world is different from ours. You have to learn about fish and understand their environment in order to fish successfully.

place close to his home, where someone caught a lot of fish a few years ago. But that was a few years ago. Now there are hardly any fish in the small pond where Tom spent his day. That was one big reason that he didn't catch anything!

People fish in the wrong places for many reasons. A pond may be close by, or may be pretty. But the prettiest thing is feeling a tug on the end of your line and knowing you've got a big one!

Some people choose a site because they have seen fish there. But seeing fish swimming around is not the same as catching and eating them. Maybe the fish are well fed, and not too eager to bite. Maybe they aren't the kind of fish you want to eat.

How do you pick a good fishing spot? Here are a few tips.

Look for a place that not many people know about. You will be surprised at how many "hidden" ponds and streams can be found with a little effort, even near big cities.

The pond where Tom didn't catch any fish was the same pond he had visited half a dozen times before. Someone once told him that big fish were biting there, and Tom kept going back.

Opposite: Sometimes you need to wade into the water so that your line will reach down into the deep areas where fish like to hide.

Many companies and factories have small lakes on their property where the fishing is good. You might see these from the highway, or a friend might tell you about them. Farms often have ponds or streams that are good for fishing. But don't trespass—ask the companies and the landowners for permission to fish. When you are finished, leave the land and water as clean as you found them.

Parks and forests have many bodies of water that can be fished, too. Of course you will not find many fish in water that is polluted, and you should not eat the ones you do find. Many edible fish live in muddy waters. Ask your state fishing agents about fish you can and cannot eat.

Talk to good fishermen about locations. Someone who says a lake "sounds good," but hasn't caught any fish there, is not a very good source of advice. The person who knows where the fish are is the person who has caught them.

You might have to "pump" your source a little bit. A fisherman who finds a good place does not want the whole world to know about it. On the other hand, fishermen do love to boast about their catches!

Check the sports pages of your local newspaper. Radio and television sports reports and programs

Opposite: Those who learn about each place they go to fish will be rewarded with a large catch and a few good meals

might help, too. Your area's fish and wildlife service office can also tell you where the fish might bite.

You might not catch anything the first few times you go fishing. When the fish finally bite, then you know you have a good place.

Pages 16-17: Half the fun of fishing is getting away to the quiet beauty of nature.

But there is more to catching fish than picking the right spot. You must choose the right bait — and go fishing at the right time. The fish should get the breakfast or dinner they like best.

17

Chapter 3

What the Fish Want

When you go out to dinner with your family, there are many places to eat. How do you decide where to go?

First, it depends on what you want to eat. Like people, different fish prefer different kinds of food. What kinds of fish live in the water where you will be fishing? Give them the food they like.

For simple pole fishing, or stillfishing, all you really need is a pole, some fishing line, a hook, and a bobber. The pole or stick should be sturdy. You will have to buy the fishing line and hook. Cotton string gets wet and breaks, and a good hook is hard to make. You might want to buy a bobber, too, but a piece of cork will do. Attach the bobber to the fishing line a few feet above the hook. It floats, or

Opposite: You need the right equipment in order to fish: fishing poles and line, bobbers, hooks and lures, tackle box, and bait.

19

"bobs," on the surface of the water. When it is pulled under, that's usually a sign that you have snagged a fish.

Most fish want to see the "menu" before they bite. They want to see—and smell—what you have on your hook. Bring along more than one kind of meal for the fish. They might not like the first thing you offer. But they might eagerly flock to the second!

Worms that you dig up in your own backyard or in a nearby field sometimes are excellent bait. Look for them under rocks and piles of old leaves, too. Minnows can be good, since large fish feed on smaller fish. You can buy minnows at a bait store. Some people use crayfish or soft-shell crabs as bait. Bits of cheese or bacon, marshmallows, or kernels of corn can even work.

Sometimes you can fool the fish with an artificial bait called a *lure*. This works best with *game* fish— bigger fish that tend to fight more, such as pike or bass. You catch them by *casting,* with a rod and reel. Hold the pole behind your head, then snap it forward toward the water. Let the line out as you cast. As soon as the line hits the water, start turning the reel handle to pull it back in.

Opposite: It takes skill and practice to land a big fish like this one. The right bait is only part of the job.

If a fish sees the lure and is interested, it might "hit" and become hooked. If not, reel in the line and cast again. In casting, as in stillfishing, the more you practice, the better you'll get.

When you and your family go out to dinner, the kind of restaurant is as important as the kind of food. Sometimes you feel like eating in a dark, quiet spot. At other times, a little noise and a lot of people are fun.

Fish like to eat in different places, too. Once you have found a good river, lake, or pond, take some time to hunt up the most popular "dining spots." Jill made three of her catches near a clump of weeds in her favorite fishing pond. She knows that fish often feed near weeds or tree stumps. They can hide there from their enemies—birds and bigger fish. Weeds or wood in the water usually mean bugs or small fish nearby for the fish to feed on.

Rocks and piers are often fish favorites. Again, they can hide and eat without fear.

There is no surefire way to know exactly where the fish will be. If you have fished for a while in one spot with no luck, move on. Or try a different bait.

You have probably been in a restaurant where the service was terrible. It took too long for someone to

Opposite: Fishing is one of the activities you can do on a camping trip. The rest of the time you can hike or explore.

take your order. Or you felt rushed through your meal. You decided you would never go back!

Fish have to be treated the right way at their "restaurants," too. Throw a tiny bit of bait in the water at the spot where you are going to put your hook. This might attract fish to the spot. If they are already nearby, it might keep them around. It's like having bread and rolls on the table right away.

You have to know how deep in the water to place your hook. Sometimes, you can find this out only by trying three or four depths. Start at about a foot or two from the bottom. Fish that are too close to the surface might be dangerous to eat. (If you catch one of these, throw it back — see Chapter 8.) Wait several minutes, and if you do not get a nibble, go a little deeper. After a while you will be fishing at the right depth — where the fish are.

Do you hold your line still? Or do you move your pole once your bait is in the water? Like so much about fishing, it depends on the kind of fish you are trying to catch. The idea is to offer your bait in a way that the fish think is natural.

You wouldn't eat dinner at eleven o'clock in the morning, would you? Well, neither would a fish. The best time to go fishing is when the fish are hungry.

Opposite: Catching a fish like this doesn't happen all the time. Big fish got that way by being smart enough not to get caught.

Most fish like to eat in the early morning and the early evening. In the middle of the day, especially when the sun is out, many fish rest and stay cool at the bottom of the water. So serve your fish their meals at sunrise and sunset. Chances are you will catch more fish.

Pages 26-27: It is harder to catch fish during the day when the sun is high in the sky. But you might get a bite in cool, shaded areas.

Chapter 4

What Are Fish Like?

You know what fish like to eat, but what are fish like? The more you know about that, the better your chances of catching them. Before you set out with your fishing pole, take the time to find out what kinds of fish live in the lake or pond where you will be fishing. Read everything you can find about them. It will help you become a better fisherman.

Fish have the same five senses as you do—sight, hearing, smell, taste, and touch. The first three senses are the most important. A fish does not touch or taste your bait until you have lured it close.

Most fish cannot see things that are very far away. But at short distances, they see very keenly. You must hide the hook completely if you are putting a worm on it.

Opposite: Some fish, like salmon, travel upstream through the rapids to mate. If you know that and fish at the right time, you can get a big catch.

Fish do not see colors as well as we do. So when you use a lure, use the brightest color you can find. Red, yellow, and white seem to be the best. But when your lure is made to look like a natural food — minnows or crayfish, for example — it should be the natural color.

Some fish can smell better than others. Those that find food on the bottom of lakes or rivers, such as catfish, have a pretty good sense of smell. Others do not. If you are trying to catch fish that can smell well, use natural bait or rub a little food from home on your lure. Many fish like the smell of liver.

Fish "hear" the vibrations of sounds through the water, not the sounds themselves. You can talk on the shore, and a fish will not know unless you are shouting. But when you hit your elbow against a boat, the vibrations will go down into the water and probably scare the fish away. But you can play a radio in the boat almost as loud as you want. The sound waves will go up into the air.

Do fish think? No, not as we do. Fish can "learn" certain lessons to go with their natural instincts. Some fish that have avoided capture for a long time learned early in life that there is danger in a dangling line, or a bright object skimming the surface.

Opposite: Fish often travel in groups called "schools" and warn each other about danger. You must not scare them if you want to catch them.

31

Chapter 5

Thinking About Fishing

Fishing is different from just about any other sport. Most of our activities are fast, fast, fast. Even when you sit and watch television, the picture changes every few seconds. Well, it isn't like that with fishing.

Tom, for instance, still has to learn that it takes *patience* to catch fish. Sometimes, hours pass before you feel that first wonderful tug at the end of your line. Once you do, many more might follow in the next few minutes. Until then, you simply must wait. You must pick the best spots, and you must keep still for long periods of time. While you are waiting, think, "The fish are there. They are

Opposite: Being patient does not have to be boring. You can talk to other fishermen on the pier and make new friends.

swimming around. Soon, one of them will notice my bait." Or, "The fish have already seen my bait. They are interested. They want to wait until just the right moment."

Pages 34-35: Sometimes it is better not to talk while you fish. It can take a lot of concentration to land fish in tricky waters.

A good fisherman waits as silently and patiently as the fish. During the wait, the good fisherman

35

keeps a keen and thoughtful eye on the water.

Watch for signs of where the fish are, and where they seem to be feeding.

Maybe you chose a spot in the shadow of a tree, because you knew that fish like to go where it is cool. But now the sun has moved, and the shadows have changed. It might be time for you to move. Do so quietly. Take your line out of the water without disturbing the area. Wait a moment before you put it in a new spot.

No matter how carefully you watch the water, there will still be times when you simply must sit and be patient. That is one of the reasons that so many people love to go fishing. They can use the time to relax, and think about whatever they want. Their cares wash away, as the water washes out from the shore.

All that time, the best fisherman does one other thing: sends out *mental waves* to the fish, telling them to come closer, closer. . . to take the bait! Strange as it seems, this can help. You are not just trying to reach the fish. You are mentally talking to *yourself*. And you are telling yourself, "I will catch fish!"

Opposite: You will not have to worry about the sun in thick forests where the leaves of the trees form an "umbrella" to keep off the sun. Remember to dress warmly.

Chapter 6

You Caught One!

You sit on the edge of a stream or pond. Or you are in a boat. The water has quieted. The wind is gone for a moment. The world seems perfectly still.

Then, suddenly, you feel something. It isn't just the motion of your line in the water. Your bobber goes under!

A fish is on your hook—or is it?

There is no doubt that a fish has taken hold of your bait and pulled it down. But is the fish hooked yet? That is a big question for every fisherman. If a fish has taken the bait, and you don't give the line a little pull to set the hook, your prey might get away. Yet if a fish is just nibbling and is not yet hooked, you will lose the fish if you move the line.

Opposite: Fish can sometimes be seen moving near the surface of the water. That will help you decide where to put your hook.

What should you do?

One reason fishing is so much fun is that each fish is different. You have to decide in a split second what to do when your bobber goes down. The more you fish, the easier it will be to decide. But you will never have a sure way to know. So do not be discouraged if you lose fish more often than you hook them. Fishing is a matter of "feel" as much as anything else, and your "feel" for it will grow with practice.

One hint: Find out before you go what kind of fish might be biting. You will know, for example, when you have hooked a big fish. It will probably pull your line so hard that the pole will seem to jump out of your hand. In that case, pull back a little, so the fish is hooked for good. But do not snap the pole too hard. The hook might be jerked right out of the fish's mouth.

Opposite: Trout fishing is very popular, because they are found in many parts of the United States and they taste very good. You could bring home a catch like this.

Chapter 7

Bringing It In

You can hook a fish firmly, pull it out of the water, and even watch it flop on the ground—without really "catching" it.

A fish is not caught until it is securely fastened on a stringer in the water or in your bucket, with the hook out of its mouth. Your fish is not dead when you pull it out of the water. In fact, fish can live out of water for longer than you might think. But it is important to remove the hook quickly and to keep the fish alive until you are sure you will keep and eat it.

When you are fishing with a simple pole, bobber, and bait, do not "fight" or "play" the fish. Bring it in as quickly as possible. Set the fish down well

Opposite: Some people go night fishing and land fish as big as these. You need to bring lanterns to help you see and keep you warm.

behind you so it cannot escape by flopping back into the water. The longer you hold the line in the air with the fish on the end, the deeper the hook might go.

The next step is to remove the hook. Fish are slippery. Their fins can cut you, and some have sharp teeth. The idea is to remove the hook with as little injury to the fish as possible. But it is important to protect yourself at the same time. Put one foot on your line a few inches from the fish. Hold the fish down with a gloved hand or a piece of cloth, cardboard, or a stick. Remove the hook with the other hand.

Do not simply pull the hook out. First, see where and how the hook has entered the fish. Does the bottom of the hook show on the outside? Is the hook embedded in the fish's jaw? If so, it might take you several minutes to pull it out properly. Work it out gently, in the opposite direction from the way it went in.

Once the hook is out, you still have not caught your fish. Make sure to put it in a pail or on a *stringer*. One end of this thick string goes through both upper and lower lips. Some stringers have separate large clasps to hold each fish. The other

Opposite: These fishermen were glad they brought a long stringer to hold their big catch. You might not be so lucky, but be prepared for anything.

end is tied fast to your boat or a strong stake on the shore.

When you are casting, you might have to fight a fish for many minutes—sometimes as long as half an hour—before you can catch it. Some game fish are strong enough to break your line or tear away from the hook. You must tire them out before you bring them in. Wait until you still feel a slight tug, but no jerking of the line. Then reel it in, quickly but

Pages 46-47: Parents and older brothers and sisters can do the catching, and little children can take charge of the fish that are caught.

steadily. Remove the hook, and put the fish in your pail or on a stringer.

Now you have caught your fish. And you are all ready to catch many more!

47

Chapter 8

Keep It?
Throw it Back?

You should throw back any fish that you do not want to eat. Do it right away.

Don't keep fish to sort out at the end of the day. Many will die if kept a few hours, then thrown back.

Remember that some fish are subject to state laws. They must be a certain size, or you may catch only a certain number each day. Know the laws that apply to you before you go fishing.

Always throw back a sick or contaminated fish. Here are some ways to recognize it:

Opposite: Game fish are wonderful to look at. Some people throw their catches back to preserve the beauty of the lake. Others mount their fish and hang them on the walls.

- It swims or floats too close to the surface.

- It swims some of the time on its side.

- It smells different from the usual "fishy" smell.

- Its skin is loose.

- Its skin is slimy, not just slippery.

- Its eyes look "loose."

- It flopped on the shore by itself.

Why should you throw back unhealthy fish? Won't they make the other fish sick?

You seldom have to worry about that. Fish get sick like any other creature, and healthy fish sense how to protect themselves. Usually, they stay away from the fish that is ill.

But why should you throw back a healthy fish if you do not want to eat it?

"One reason," Jill says, "is so it will be there next time!"

Another reason is that it is the fair way. There is no point to killing a good fish if you are not going to eat it.

Opposite: The healthiest fish live in clean, clear lakes and streams. Don't fish in water that doesn't look good.

Chapter 9

Now What?

You have caught your fish. Maybe you caught a lot of fish. What do you do next?

The first thing you do is look at all of them, decide how many — and which ones — you will eat. Then throw the rest back.

You might want to prepare a fish or two right on shore. There is hardly anything in the world that tastes as good as a freshly caught and cooked fish. If you are planning to cook outdoors, be sure to bring some butter, salt, and pepper, and anything else you want to eat with your fish.

Put the rest of your catch in a bucket of water. You do not want them to spoil before you get home. At home, prepare them or freeze them for later.

Fish must be gutted and skinned or at least scaled

Opposite: A full day of fishing can really work up an appetite. Cooking and eating the fish is a tasty reward for the effort.

before they can be cooked. With a sharp knife, make a cut in the belly of the fish from gills to anal vent. Open the fish, remove everything except meat and bones. Run your thumb up and down the base of the cleaned cavity to remove dark material (blood) there. The "guts" of a fish can be unhealthy and even poisonous to eat.

You can also buy a tool called a *scaler* at just about any sporting goods or bait store. Move the scaler back and forth along the outside of the fish, firmly but not too hard. Soon the scales will come off. A large, firm spoon will do, too, as will a knife edge.

Even if you plan to freeze your fish, gut and scale them soon after you catch them. If you do not, the fish might spoil.

Fish can be cooked in a number of ways. How you cook your fish depends on your taste. Some fish seem better fried, others broiled. Some fishermen remove the bones and skin, and cut their fish into fillets.

Be careful to cook your fish well. The head should not be eaten, but you can leave it on when you prepare the fish for cooking.

Mmmm. . . can't you just taste that freshly cooked fish?

Opposite: Fish cook very quickly in a cast-iron skillet. Turn them often so they will not burn.

Chapter 10

A Final "Fish Story"

There was once a fish called Old Bob. Old Bob was the largest, wisest fish in the small lake near the town where Jill and Tom live. Once, when Old Bob was younger, a fisherman hooked him. But the fish wriggled free. After that, Old Bob was too smart ever to take the bait. Once in a while, he would jump out of the water in the middle of the lake. Fishermen would yell, "Look! Look! It's Old Bob!"

Just seeing Old Bob was better than catching any other fish.

Then one day, something happened. A few families were going fishing. They asked a newcomer in town, Ralph, to come along. Ralph had never fished before, and did not feel very sure of himself. His friends told him not to worry. It was all right if he didn't catch anything.

Opposite: Hooking that smart fish is challenging and exciting!

So Ralph went fishing for the first time. And almost by accident, he hooked Old Bob!

There was more excitement than the town had ever seen. But no one wanted to eat Old Bob. After all, he was a living legend! With the help of his friends, Ralph drove the fish to the state capital. There, Old Bob was put in a big aquarium.

Almost everyone in town made the trip to see Old Bob. But the strange thing was, they came back sad. They did't want to go again. Even though Ralph was a pretty nice fellow, whenever he started talking about Old Bob, people would suddenly drift away.

One day the truth hit Ralph. Old Bob didn't belong in a fish tank. He belonged in the lake where he had lived all his life.

Ralph returned to the aquarium. He asked if he could please have Old Bob back. Finally, he put the grand fish back in the lake.

Ralph did not tell anyone. Instead, he asked his friends to go out fishing. At first, they did not want to. Whenever they thought of fishing and Ralph, they thought of Old Bob in that aquarium. But Ralph promised there would be a big surprise.

So one day Jill and Tom and a few of their friends grabbed their poles and went with Ralph. They had been fishing about twenty minutes when Old Bob did just what Ralph knew he would do.

He leaped out of the water in the middle of the lake. He said hello to the town again!

"Old Bob! I think I just saw Old Bob!" shrieked Jill.

"No, it can't be," her brother said.

"But I saw him, too! It was Old Bob!" Tom shouted.

Ralph smiled. "It *was* Old Bob," he said proudly. And then he told them how he had brought Old Bob back to the lake.

The town was happy again.

And so was Old Bob.

It is good to have aquariums and zoos so we can see living creatures we might never get another chance to look at.

But some things do not belong in captivity.

Each living thing is an individual, different from any other, just like people—even though some of them look very much the same on the outside.

Once in a while, you might get to know one of these living things so well that it becomes like a person to you.

When you feel that, you know what is most important about catching fish. They are a part of nature, just as you are.

For Further Reading

Fabian, John, *Fishing for Beginners,* 1st ed., New York: Atheneum, 1974.

Farmer, Charles J., *Creative Fishing,* Harrisburg, Pa.: Stackpole Books, 1973.

Liss, Howard, *Fishing Talk for Beginners,* New York: J. Messner, 1978.

Marsnall, Mel, *How to Fish: A Commonsense Approach,* New York: Winchester Press, 1978.

McNally, Tom, *Fishing,* Chicago: Follett, 1972.

Meyers, Chet, *Catching Fish,* Minneapolis: Dillon Press, 1978.

Sand, George X., *The Complete Beginner's Guide to Fishing,* 1st ed., Garden City, N.Y.: Doubleday, 1974.

Selsam, Millicent (Ellis), *A First Look at Fish,* New York: Walker, 1972.

Stokes, William F., *You Can Catch Fish,* Milwaukee: Raintree Editions, 1976.

Swayne, Dick, *I Am A Fisherman,* Philadelphia: Lippincott, 1978.

The Rules of Fishing

Here are some important rules to learn if you want to be a success at fishing:

- Buy a license if your state requires one.
- Know where the fish are, and fish when they are hungry.
- Don't trespass — ask the landowners for permission to fish on their property.
- Leave the land and water the way you found them.
- Find out which kinds of fish live in your fishing spot and learn everything you can about them.
- Bring along more than one kind of meal for the fish.
- Remove the hook carefully so that you don't hurt yourself or the fish.
- Don't eat fish from dirty water or fish that look sick, and throw back any fish you aren't going to eat.
- Clean and scale the fish you are going to keep right away, and always cook the fish completely.
- Learn whatever you can from other fishermen and practice what you learn.
- Wait as silently and patiently as the fish and keep a keen and thoughtful eye on the water.

Index